who

Free Stuff

The Insider's Guide to Free Products and Making Money from Home

$ $ $

Bruce Lub

Dedication

To our boys, our favorite work-at-home opportunity.

Please note:

At press time, all of these offers were still valid, but they won't be forever! Free offers change frequently, so don't be surprised if something inside this book is no longer available. Try poking around the site listed to see if you can find the offer elsewhere. Or let us know that something has expired by visiting WhoKnewTips.com, and we'll do our best to find you a similar free offer or
work-from-home opportunity.

The offers in this book have been pre-screened, but for your protection, please make sure to carefully investigate any free offers or work-at-home opportunities before you accept. Be wary of giving out your credit card information and especially your social security number, which you should never have to provide for a free offer. For a list of fraudulent work-at-home offers from the Federal Trade Regulation, please visit FTC.gov/bcp/menus/consumer/invest/workhome.shtm.

Contents

CHAPTER 1

Free Money!

Who doesn't love free money? Whether you're need help with your down payment, looking to get cash for your old phone or gadget, want to make money back just for shopping online, or more, this chapter is for you! Discover how easy it is to get a little money here and there for the small things, and how to collect tons of money-saving coupons while you're at it.

Small Business Help

The Association for Enterprise Opportunity is an association of organizations committed to small businesses. On their site, you'll find plenty of information about the grants and other resources that are available for the budding entrepreneur. You can find it all at MicroEnterpriseWorks.org.

Down Payments for Your Home

Most down payment programs were phased out in 2008, so be wary if you come across a website offering a deal that's too good to be true (it probably is). However, other grant money is still available. Just go to DownPaymentSolutions.com and click on "Grants" to find out if you qualify for any free money that will help you purchase a house, co-op, or condo.

Money for College

These days, college can cost $10,000–$50,000 for one year! And that's just for a bachelor's degree. The good news is that there is a lot of free money out there, from grants and scholarships to assistantships and fellowships. Here are some ways to find it.

- FedMoney.org is probably the most comprehensive online resource on all US government grants and student financial aid programs. Here, you will find detailed information about who can apply and how for more than 130 government grants and loans related to education. You can also check the US Department of Education's site at StudentAid.ed.gov.
- At Upromise.com, you can earn money toward your children's college educations—or help pay off student loan debt already accrued—through your everyday purchases. Register your credit/debit cards along with cards from grocery and

drug store reward programs, and then earn points for every purchase you make at thousands of retailers nationwide.

- To find out all about grants (and how to get them), make sure to visit CollegeScholarships.org/grants.
- Check out PrincetonReview.com or Petersons.com to find searchable lists of grants from the lofty (a National Merit scholarship) to the small and silly ($500 for speaking Klingon).
- For local awards and scholarship contests, make sure to check the newspaper and at the high school counselor's office for opportunities.
- If you know what college your son or daughter is attending, make sure you have an up-to-date list of all merit- and need-based grants and loans it offers. If you think you may qualify, don't be afraid to call up the school's registrar or financial aid department and ask for more information.

Help with Your Utility Bills

The Low Income Home Energy Assistance Program (LIHEAP) helps pay heating and electricity costs of low-income and elderly people. You can enroll in the program whether you rent or own, and you don't necessarily need to be receiving other government assistance to qualify. Each state's program is different, so for more information, go to ACF.HHS.gov and click on "Energy Assistance" for details.

Life Insurance

Free life insurance? It's true: Mass Mutual offers free premiums for a life insurance policy with a $50,000 death benefit if you quality. You must be between 19 and 42, be the parent or legal guardian of one or more children under the age of 18, and also meet specific financial criteria. For details go to search for "Lifebridge

SM" online, and enter "free premiums" in the search bar or call 1-800-272-2216.

Re: Rebates

Find loads of items on sale near you that are free after a mail-in rebate. Just visit SalesCircular.com. Click on your state of residence and you'll be directed to a list of products by type—electronics, apparel, appliances, etc.—that are on sale in your area. Click on "Free after rebate" and get a list of items that you can get for free, from make-up to software.

Free Coupons!

Coupons aren't just for people who buy the Sunday paper anymore! There is now an impressive array of coupon sites online that offer coupons on groceries, household items, toys, and more. Here are some of our favorites.

- At Eversave.com, they search for the best deals, or "Saves," in your ZIP code on everything from hair cuts to yoga classes. When you sign up with their site they will send you an email every day letting you know about the latest Save and allowing you to easily share it with your friends.
- Perhaps our all-time favorite site for savings is CouponMom. com, where you can save time and money by matching your store's weekly sales items with coupons available from the Sunday newspaper or online websites. What's so unique about this site is it provides a list of the best grocery deals and coupons by state. So, if you're interested in what's on sale at, say, Shop Rite in New Jersey, for example, each week's offerings are noted here. In addition, the site provides a "Virtual coupon organizer," which will help you organize coupons you've pulled from around the web.

- At Taylortown Coupon Preview (TaylortownPreview.com), you can get a sneak peek at upcoming coupons that will appear in your Sunday paper and other publications, along with an ever-changing array of free offers.
- Some of the easiest coupons to print out can be found at Coupons.com, where you can search and easily print out coupons after downloading a simple program. You can also select coupons to be added directly to your grocery store's customer rewards program, so you don't even need to print anything out. Just click on the coupon and you'll get the discount when you use your card.

Why Pay for Shipping?

Many online retailers offer free shipping if you can pick up your order at one of their stores, including Walmart.com, REI.com, and Payless.com. This is especially handy for online-only items, oversize purchases (which will cost a lot to ship), or goods that have sold out at your local store. Also, look for free shipping deals at many sites when you spend a certain amount, such as orders over $25 at Amazon.com. Find even more deals at FreeShipping.org.

Know the Code

Ever go to buy something online and see that little box to enter a promotional or coupon code? Well now you never have to wish you had something to enter into that box again. At RetailMeNot.com, you can find hundreds of codes that will give you savings at a large variety of websites, including Kohls.com, Amazon.com, and JC Penney online. If this site doesn't have a code for the store you're looking for, also try MomsView.com, DealTaker.com, or PocketDeal.com. Or simply type the name of the online store you need and the word "coupon code" into a search engine.

Fatten Your Wallet

Even if trolling the internet for coupons isn't your bag, there is still one site you definitely need to sign up at: FatWallet.com. Signing up at FatWallet is one of the best ways to start saving money online immediately and easily. All you have to do is log on to the site before making purchases at such websites as BabiesRUs.com, Payless shoes, Nordstrom.com, Buy.com, and Walmart. They'll give you money back on everything you buy—usually 2–8 percent, and let you know if there are any coupon codes for sales on the site. You can even earn cash back for using travel sites like Hotels.com, Expedia.com, and JetBlue.com, and if you use an online dating site, you can save a huge portion on your membership (Match.com gives you 30 percent back and Chemistry.com 50 percent!). You'll usually have to wait several months for your money, but when it's as simple as clicking through, why not? (For more details on how it all works, check out their FAQ page.) And if you do enjoy coupon clipping, they also offer printable coupons and one of the best user forums about recent deals on the web.

Ebates Are the New Rebates

Get free cash back just for shopping online at Ebates.com. Before you shop at your favorite sites (including HomeDepot.com, BN.com, Kohls.com, Target.com, and more), just log in at Ebates.com first. Then click through to your desired website. You get a certain percentage of cash back on each site, and a check will be mailed to you every three months. It's that easy!

Does a Company Owe You Money?

Hundreds of lawsuits are settled every day, entitling purchasers of products to money they don't even know about. At TopClassActions.com, find easy-to-navigate lists of recent settlements and how to get money from them. During one recent visit, we found out Costco owed us a free three-month membership and anyone with AT&T internet service could get $2.90 for every month they had subscribed!

Savings Bonds You May Not Know About

Did you know that more than 25,000 mature savings bonds aren't cashed each year? To find out if there is a bond in your name that you didn't know or have forgotten about, check out TreasuryHunt.gov or call 800-722-2678.

Lost Money Could Be Yours!

There is over $24 billion worth of unclaimed property in the United States, and Unclaimed.org is the official government site to find out if any of it is yours. Search by name and state, and be connected to federal and state databases to see if there is any money, land, or possessions that have been left to you and are in government custody.

Is Your Old Computer Worth Something?

Go to Apple.com/recycling to find out if your old computer (Mac or PC) is worth anything! If Apple can use the parts, they'll pay you in the form of an Apple gift card. You can also get 10% off an iPod by bringing your old one into an Apple store.

Cash for Your Gadgets

Now you can keep your old electronics out of the landfill and possibly get some free cash in exchange! Services such as BuyMyTronics.com and Gazelle.com recycle or refurbish your old cast-offs and send you a check in return. Just fill out the easy forms on their websites. They'll make you an offer, and if you accept, send you a box with postage to send your gizmo to them. They take cameras, cell phones, MP3 players, game consoles, personal computers, and more.

Get Money for Your Ink Cartridges

Got empty cartridges for a printer, copier, or fax machine? TonerBuyer.com will buy them from you, and even pay the shipping! Fill out their online form to find out how much your cartridges are worth, then print out the prepaid mailing form and wait for your check in the mail. You can also print empty printer cartridges into Staples stores, which will get you a $2 credit (up to 10 cartridges a month).

What to Do with Unwanted Gift Cards

Has that gift card to Smitty's Bird Bath Emporium that your aunt gave you been sitting on your desk for years? Head over to PlasticJungle.com or GiftCardRescue.com to get cash from unused gift cards! They'll pay you a portion of the total cost of your card (around 80–90%) and resell it on their site. If you've purchased a deal from a site like Groupon or Living Social that you now realize you're not going to use before it expires, check out CoupRecoup.com, where you can sell your purchased deals to someone who will use them.

Money for Your Old Phone

If you're buying a new cell phone, what do you do with the old one? Get cash, of course! Visit Cell4Cash.com and enter the brand and model of your old phone. The site will tell you if they're offering any money for it, and if they're not, they still allow you to send it in to be recycled. Plus, the shipping is free!

Sell Your Used Sporting Goods

OK, so you tried to get the kids into tennis, and it never worked. Instead of letting the racquets (and any other unused sports equipment) gather dust at the back of your closet, take them into Play It Again Sports and get cash or store credit. (To find stores near you, visit PlayItAgainSports.com.) You can also try out UsedSports.com, which allows you to list your sporting equipment at any price you choose.

CHAPTER 2

Work-from-Home Opportunities

Who knew that 3.5 percent of the nation's workforce works from home, and more than 8 million US workers hold two or more jobs? If you need a boost to your income, or just a little extra cash, check out these work-from-home opportunities. Make money just for your opinion, evaluate websites and court cases from your home computer, find out how to sell homemade items and things you no longer need, discover the different products you can sell to friends, and more. Best of all, you probably won't even need to change out of your pajamas!

Selling Cosmetics

If you love make-up, selling Avon or Mary Kay cosmetics may be for you—especially since you'll great a great discount on their products that you can use yourself. Both companies require that you cover all costs, but Avon's initial set-up fee is lower. And while Mary Kay usually offers a higher commission on sales, they may require you to purchase inventory before you sell it. If you're trying to decide whether Avon or May Kay would be a better fit for you, the biggest factor to consider may simply be which company's product you and your friends prefer. Not only will you be able to sell it better, but if your friends use it you know you'll have at least a few sales. Ask around and see if there are already a lot of reps from one company or the other in your area—if there are a lot of "Avon ladies" in your neighborhood or at your primary workplace, you might want to consider Mary Kay. Also keep in mind that Mary Kay's prices are higher, so if you don't see your friends spending a lot on make-up, Avon may be the better choice. One friend who has sold for both companies summed it up by telling us that if you just want to be a casual seller, Avon is your best bet. But if you're willing to give it your all, you can probably make more money with Mary Kay.

When "Jury Duty" Is a Good Thing

Did you know that many trial lawyers present their arguments to "mock juries" before their case appears before a judge? Gauging the reactions of everyday Americans helps lawyers build stronger cases, and they want your help. If you're an American citizen over the age of 18 who has never been convicted of a felony, you qualify! Just go to www.TrialJuries.com and click on "Sign up" to be included in their database of prospective mock jurors. If you're chosen, you'll get around $30 to review audio, pictures, and text evidence and answer a questionnaire.

Have Something to Teach? How About Tutoring?

If you know how to play an instrument or have a background in math, science, or English, tutoring may be a good way to make some extra cash. Put up flyers in your area, post an ad on Craigslist.org, and talk to local schools and after-school programs to see if they have children in need of tutoring. Make sure to have your résumé handy, and provide references, even if they're in the form of your friends whose children you have taught a skill. If you have a bachelor's degree and a fast internet connection, you can also sign up to be a tutor at EduWizards.com.

Online Teachers Wanted!

At Limu.com, people who know things are connected with those who want to know them! Set up an online class in your subject area using Limu's virtual classroom, and you even get to decide how much to charge per online student. You can also browse their listings of "wanted knowledge assets"—skills and knowledge people are looking to learn—and see if any of your skills match. For more information, visit Limu.com/pages/teach.html.

Help Others Learn English

Sign up at Idapted.com and you can help students learn English just by talking to them through your computer! You'll need a fast internet connection and a headset, and to complete Idapted's certification process. Then, simply log on to walk students through guided lesson plans that consist mostly of just having a conversation in English. You can earn up to $10 an hour, and can get pay increases based on students' ratings.

Test Websites

Help web developers find out the ways in which their websites are confusing or not working well by becoming a website tester for UserTesting.com. They'll give you software to install on your computer that tracks your mouse's movements, and ask you to narrate a short video while you use the site. After answering a few questions, you'll be paid $10 per site you review. To find out more information, visit UserTesting.com/BeTester.

Focus Groups

When they need to know what real people think about their products, companies hire focus groups to try them and then share their opinions. Being in a focus group can get you free product samples, a bit of cash, and the opportunity for your voice to be heard! Sign up to be part of a focus group at FGGlobal. com, where you enter information about yourself and then receive emails when there is focus group work available in your area. Or go to FindFocusGroups.com, which culls focus group opportunities from around the web that you can apply for directly. Either way, you should know that many focus groups won't hire you if you work in the marketing industry, have any connection to the company the product is made by, or say that you have participated in a focus group in the last six months.

Mystery Shopping (Because You've Always Been the Mysterious Type)

Mystery shopping can get you free products and a bit of money on the side, but most of all it's downright fun. Visit a store, then fill out an online survey about your experience. The pay isn't much—usually not more than $15—but you'll be reimbursed for products as varied as designer sunglasses to lunch and a beer at a restaurant. If you're interested in mystery shopping, be careful of online scams. You should never have to pay to be a mystery shopper! Check out one of our favorite mystery shopping services, GAPbuster.com/mysteryshop, or search for mystery shopping and focus group opportunities near you at MysteryShop.org/shoppers, which is run by the Mystery Shopping Providers Association.

To Get Your Fifteen Minutes of Fame... and Maybe Some Cash!

Ever wanted to see if you could win some money on TV? Go to StarNow.com or TalentSubmit.com to search for opportunities in your area to be a movie or TV extra, try out for a reality show, or be a guest on a talk show. And don't forget us when you become famous!

Make It a Party: Selling Tupperware or Other Products

If you're a friendly person with lots of contacts, selling products could be the perfect way for you to make some extra cash. We've all heard of Tupperware parties, but there are now a lot more products available for you to sell from home. Most require that you pay an initial start-up fee, which usually includes some samples and catalogs, and all the programs offer extra incentives like freebies and bonuses for meeting certain sales goals. Below is a run-down of some of the opportunities available, and how to find out more information.

- The grandmother of all work-from-home sales opportunities, Tupperware is now much more than parties. For a small fee, you can also get your own website from which to sell Tupperware items. The commission is usually 25 percent of everything you sell, and you need to sell about $100 worth of items per month for Tupperware to keep you on. If you think you can recruit friends to become Tupperware representatives, all the better! You get a portion of their sales, too, and if you recruit enough people, Tupperware will promote you to manager and you'll get an even bigger cut. Tupperware gives you two choices of starter kits: one for $80 and one for $120. For more info, visit Tupperware.com or contact your local representative.
- The Pampered Chef has been selling high-quality kitchen products since 1980. As a Pampered Chef consultant, most of your sales would be done by hosting parties in your own home or the homes of your friends—so if you're a good cook, this could be a great chance to show off your skills using Pampered Chef products, feed your friends, and hopefully make a few bucks while you're at it. To get a start-up kit it will cost you $100, and the company offers a 20 percent commission, which goes up slightly if you refer two or more people. Call 1-800-266-5562 or visit PamperedChef.com for more information.
- If you and your friends are into scrapbooking, then Stampin' Up might be for you. Their starter kit of stamps, pads, and other stamping doodads costs $200, but the great thing about this program is that your compensation goes up according to how much you sell per month. Sell up to $400 per month and you'll receive 20 percent of all your orders, but sell more than $5,000

per month and you'll earn 40 percent. Visit StampinUp.com for more details.

- If you can't get enough of candles, try Partylite. They have no monthly minimum that you need to sell, and you can get a free starter kit when you host your first show. They'll also set you up with your own website for $10 per month. As with many other programs, you get more money the more Partylite representatives you refer. For information on how to sign up, go to Partylite.com.

- If you have kids, you know that there's no end to the amount of kids' toys one can buy. So head over to DiscoveryToysInc. com, where you can find information about how to sell fun, educational products for children. They provide you with videos and instructions to help you get started, and charge $99 for a beginner's kit. You'll make 20 percent of every sale, and only need to sell $150 worth of products every three months.

- These are just a few of the opportunities available to you if you would like to start selling items from home! For a directory of even more opportunities and everything you need to know about joining up with various companies (including how to claim it on your taxes), visit DirectSelling411.com.

Easily Sell Handmade Items

Are you a crafter? A knitter? A genius with paper mache? Etsy.com will give you a worldwide venue to sell your item. Sign up for free and get your very own virtual shop, then pay 20¢ for every item you list. You can set the price at whatever you want, and when it sells, you pay Etsy 3.5 percent of the price to handle the credit card transaction. You can also be featured on the Etsy.com home page for an extra fee, which is visited by thousands of people looking to buy handmade items.

Good with Animals?

No matter what shape the economy is in, people will always need dog-walkers and cat-sitters. Both jobs can get you $10–$20 an hour, and you'll get to spend time with some furry friends (who will never drink the last of the coffee in the office kitchenette). The trick to this business is to get a lot of clients in close proximity to each other, so you don't have to spend a lot of time and money on travel. Try advertising at pet stores, groomers', and veterinary offices near you. Don't forget to list your pets as references!

The Survey Says...

The folks at SurveySpot.com not only want your opinion, they'll pay for it. Join for free and you'll receive 5–7 surveys each week to complete. For each completed survey, they'll pay you $2–$10 or enter you in a sweepstakes (or both!). This and other survey sites like MySurvey.com, EPoll.com, and Toluna.com can be frustrating because you don't always qualify to take the survey and it can take a while to earn money, but if you enjoy answering questions and have a bit of free time, this is a great way to earn some extra cash while you're messing around on the web.

Extra Money for Photographers

If you have a gift for taking beautiful photographs, there may be a side career for you in photography. Advertise your services to become a wedding and special events photographer, and make some extra dough on the weekends—just make sure you have a sophisticated web site where people can view your work. You can also make money selling your images to publishers and creative professionals who are looking for stock photography. Go to Shutterpoint.com, Dreamstime.com, or iStockPhoto.com to find out more about selling your images online.

Writing for a Living

If you're a good writer and have a love for your local community, why not share your knowledge with others for a little cash? Examiner.com regularly hires writers to write about events and community interest articles from around town. Just go to Examiner.com and click on "Write for us." DemandStudios.com (which supplies articles to eHow.com) also hires writers, as well as copyeditors and videographers. The base pay isn't much, but you'll get more money as you get more hits to your page.

Great Job for Friendly People

Dressing up as a sandwich and handing out flyers is a tough job, but somebody's got to do it. Actually, getting a job with a "street team" company doesn't require that you get dressed up (usually). They hire outgoing people to hand out flyers on the street and in bars that promote a new album, an upcoming event, or newly released films. Best yet, by becoming part of a street team, you can earn $15–$25 an hour! To find out more and to sign up for a street team in your area, visit StreetTeamPromotion.jobs.

Operating a Call Center

There are many opportunities available for becoming a customer service representatives right in your own home. Sign up with Alpine Access (AlpineAccess.com), Arise Virtual Solutions (WillowCSN.com), or West Corporation (West.com) and you'll receive calls from customers needing help from major organizations like Sears, Office Depot, and the IRS. You usually need to provide your own computer with a high speed internet connection, and sometimes an extra phone line, but you'll make up to $14 an hour and won't even have to change out of your pajamas.

Renting Household Items

If you have a household item you use rarely (or need extra cash fast), how about renting it? Zilok.com allows you to rent out your car, vacation home, tools, camera, lawn mower, TV, video game console, and more. (Unfortunately, you can't rent out your kids.) For more information, go to US.Zilok.com/support.

Go for the Gold

With the value of gold so high these days, now is the time to get rid of your old gold! Take a look through your jewelry box for broken pieces and items you no longer wear. As long as they're 10 karats or higher, you can get big money for them. Just make sure you're dealing with a reputable gold broker. Never mail in your scrap gold—make sure to talk to someone in person at a jewelry or coin store. Use the online calculator at Dendritics.com/scales/metal-calc.asp to find out how much your gold is worth, and expect to get about 75–85 percent of that amount from a broker.

Have Space? Get Money!

Renting out a spare room has long been a way for families to make ends meet in tough times. But even if you don't want someone else living in your home, you may be able to rent out storage space in your garage. If you live near a train station or in a densely populated area, you may also want to think about renting out your driveway for a parking space. Place an ad on Craigslist.org or in your local paper and see if you get any bites.

CHAPTER 3

Free Stuff!

King Gillette, the inventor of the disposable razor, was unsuccessful at selling his invention until he started giving the razors away for free. Soon, everyone wanted to buy the disposable blades! Now, companies often give away free products. In fact, it's estimated that many companies send out between 5,000 and 20,000 samples of new products when they've decided to run a freebie promotion. We've made it easier than ever for you to discover these freebies, most of which are offered online. Can't find a particular freebie we've mentioned? Contact us by going to WhoKnewTips.com and we'll search for a similar sample being offered elsewhere.

Free Cosmetics and Accessories

Alluring Freebies!

At Allure.com/freestuff, find make-up and other female-centric giveaways from *Allure* magazine. Though you aren't guaranteed the freebies you sign up for (you're entered into a contest), they have full-size samples and irresistible giveaways like 42 bottles of OPI nail polishes and free haircuts for life.

Beauty Products

If you like quality skin- and hair-care products, you'll love Aveda. Sign up for their email mailing list at Aveda.com, and you'll receive free samples and offers, like a free facial at one of their retail stores.

All Kinds of Cosmetics

FreeCosmeticWebsites.com compiles free online offers from high-end manufacturers and other beauty sites. Find great deals on make-up from Revlon, Maybelline, Clinque, MAC, Bobbi Brown, and other name-brand companies, in addition to the freebies.

Make-Up

Hooray for going green! Many cosmetics retailers now offer free products in return for bringing in empty make-up containers. M.A.C., for instance, will give you a free lipstick for returning six M.A.C. containers, while Lush will give you a free face mask for every five Lush containers you bring back empty. Kiehl's has a special card just for recycling Kiehl's containers, and has various rewards depending on the number of empty containers you return. Origins has to have our favorite recycling program, though. Bring in a container from *any* make-up (regardless of brand) and get a free Origins skin-care sample!

Moisturizers and Soap

Keep your skin soft and smooth with free samples and coupons at Oil of Olay (Olay.com/samplesandoffers) and Dove (Dove.us/#/Offers/freesamples). You can also sign up for email newsletters that will keep you apprised of deals and special offers.

More Freebies for the Ladies

Vocalpoint.com is a home and lifestyle website that offers freebies in their "Try and tell" section. The freebies are great, but to access them, you'll have to become a Vocalpoint member, and they don't accept just anybody. If you're a woman and you have kids, however, you may be in luck! Click on "Become a member" to see if you qualify, then browse their freebies that range from shampoo to diet supplements.

Sephora Products

Sephora offers a wide variety of name-brand beauty products, but their real deals are their own line of cosmetics. Get a free birthday gift simply for registering for their "Beauty Insider" program. The gift varies from year to year, but you'll be sure to get a high-quality bath product, cosmetic, or skin-care item. Go to Sephora.com and click on "Sign up for Sephora" to register.

Free Jewelry!

Believe it or not, you can get free jewelry with no catches—all you have to do is pay the $6 shipping fee! SilverJewelryClub.com allows you to pick the necklaces, earrings, and other jewelry you want, then ships it to you for only $6. The amazing thing about this site is that the pieces really are quality items made from sterling silver and real gemstones, and they have so many pretty options, you'll want them all! Luckily, the site not only allows you to pick as many free items as you want, you can come back again for more! In return, all they ask is that you consider shopping at their full (not free) site, Peora.com.

FREE FOOD AND RECIPES

Recipe Book

Get a free recipe book filled with recipes from the makers of Jiffy mixes. Whether it's dinner or dessert, you'll love their delicious ideas. To fill out a form to get your free recipe book, go to JiffyMix.com and click on "Recipes," then "Order our recipe book."

Slow Cooker eBook

If you love winter slow cooker meals as much as we do, head to DivineDinnerparty.com. Get a free Crock-Pot cooking eBook just for signing up for the site's free newsletter that's full of fun hints.

The Best Place for Recipes

Our favorite site for free recipes is Epicurious.com, where you can get search for recipes by type (appetizers, drinks, entrees, etc.), or type in keywords to search for specific recipes. Since their recipes are pulled from publications like *Bon Appétit* and *Gourmet*, you know they're going to be good, but if you're not sure, you can read reader reviews. You can also start a "recipe box" of your favorite recipes from the site—make sure to include one of their more than 400 recipes for chocolate cake!

More from Kraft

At KraftFirstTaste.com, you can sign up to sample new products from Kraft Foods. After registering with the site, click on the "My offers" section to see what freebies are available. You'll have to answer a survey to get your freebies, and like most freebie sites with surveys, you'll have to answer "correctly" if you want your free sample. For example, if you say you never buy cream cheese, you probably won't be eligible to receive a free sample of Philadelphia cream cheese!

Just Like Coffee

What is Teeccino? It's an herbal coffee substitute that's perfect for people who can't have caffeine or are bothered by coffee's acidity. To get a free sample, go to Teeccino.com and subscribe to their email newsletter of healthful tips.

Nutritional Supplement

Visit Ensure.com/coupons-samples-promotions for coupons to get discounted packs of Ensure nutritional drink.

Baby Food

If you're a parent on a budget, you know every bit counts. Get a free day's supply of organic baby food at ParentsChoiceFormula.com.

C is for Energy

Get a free sample of Emergen-C energy drink by visiting Emergenc.com. Just click on "Free samples" and subscribe to their email newsletter to receive your free sample by mail.

Low-Carb Energy Bars

If you're trying to lose weight (and who isn't?) pick up a free "Quick-Start Guide" for the Atkins diet along with three free Atkins bars. Visit Atkins.com and click on the "Free Weight Loss Kit" offer.

Free Discounts on Healthy Eating

If your family likes to eat healthily (or tries to), a great site for savings is EatBetterAmerica.com. Run by General Mills, it offers free recipes as well as coupons on healthy General Mills products such as Yoplait yogurt, Nature Valley granola bars, Fiber One cereal, and Progresso soups. They also offer coupons on household items like diapers, air fresheners, mouthwash, lotion, cat food, and much more. What we love about these coupons is that they aren't the piddly little 25¢-off variety—most are worth at least 50¢, and many are for $1 or more.

Free from Betty Crocker

If you love making desserts, check out BettyCrocker.com/coupons-promotions. As you may have guessed from the web address, this site contains coupons, contests, and freebies from

Betty Crocker brands. In addition to their delicious cake and brownie mixes, you'll find deals from Bisquick, Green Giant, and Hamburger Helper. They even have a free iPhone application!

Cup of Coffee

Donut-lovers, rejoice! Dunkin' Donuts now has a reward program in many areas, and you earn a free cup of coffee just for signing up! Go to www.DDPerks.com and register for a rewards card that allows you to get free food and drinks when you use money that you've loaded on your card.

Tea

If you love tea, you'll love Adagio Teas (Adagio.com), which offers free tea rewards for buying tea, writing reviews, and sending coupons to friends. The site, which carries the widest variety of tea we've ever seen, also runs special promotions like their cool Earth Day program that allowed customers to sponsor a tea tree, then receive free tea from it once it was ready to harvest.

Chocolate!

If you're a chocoholic, your next stop online should be Godiva. com/rewards, where you can register for Godiva Chocolatier's member rewards program. Just for signing up, you'll receive a free chocolate every time you walk into a Godiva store! (Limit one per month.) You'll also get free gifts when you buy chocolate online and in-store. Make sure to log in on the 16th of each month, when you get an additional freebie when you order online.

Dinner

OpenTable.com is not only convenient for making reservations at thousands of restaurants nationwide, they also give you freebies! Earn points each time you make a reservation, then redeem them for a free meal at any of their partner restaurants. Another great site for getting money back on meals out is RewardsNetwork.com. They give you points and money back on your tab at restaurants nationwide.

Goodies from T.G.I. Friday's

Sign up for T.G.I. Friday's rewards program and you'll get a coupon for a free appetizer or dessert immediately! You'll also get points toward free food every time you dine there. To sign up and for more information, visit TGIFridays.com and click on "Give me more stripes."

Make it a Happy Birthday…

…with a free entree from Houlihan's restaurant. To join their email club at Houlihans.com, click on "Talk to Us," and then click on "Wanna Freebie." You'll also get a free appetizer just for joining.

Burritos

Burritos more to your liking? Then check out the e-club at Moe's Southwest Grill. On your birthday, they'll give you a free burrito. Other free swag comes with the membership, too. Check it out at Moes.com—just click on "Join Moe's e-World."

Smoothie and More!

Just for joining the Orange Julius "OJ Quench Club" at OrangeJulius.com/sec_quenchclub.html, you'll receive a free

20-ounce fruit drink or smoothie at one of their retail locations, and a special gift on your birthday.

We All Scream

Interested in a free three-scoop sundae from Friendly's restaurant? Just join their BFF program at Friendlys.com, and next time you buy an adult entree, leave room for your free dessert. You can also participate in some of their free birthday offers just for joining.

—Toni Belle

More Free Food

At Schlotzsky's Bun & Fun e-club you can get a free small sandwich when you sign up. And you get to tell your friends you belong to something called the "Bun & Fun club"! Just go to Schlotzskys. com and click on "Fun." (Not every restaurant participates; call locations near you to make sure.)

Qdite a Deal at Qdoba

Join Qdoba restaurant's e-club and you'll get a free entree when you buy a second entree and special deals on your birthday. You'll also enjoy free chips and salsa simply for signing up! Join by going to Qdoba.com and clicking on "Qdoba Rewards."

Free For Your Kids and Pets

What Free Stuff to Expect When You're Expecting

There are a plethora of websites featuring free stuff for newborns. If you're expecting, make sure to check these out.

- At BabiesOnline.com/offers you'll find loads of free offers and discount coupons for mothers-to-be. They have free magazines, formula samples, coupons for baby food, contests to win free diapers for a year, and more. All you have to do is check off the offers you want, then fill out your name, address, and due date.
- Type "Enfamil Family Beginnings" into a search engine, then click on the first link to get checks for free formula, baby supplies, and contests.
- Go to FitPregnancy.com/freebies to find sweepstakes and freebies from the popular magazine *Fit* and from around the web.
- At VeryBestBaby.com, you can get coupons, samples, and information about every stage of your baby's development from the makers of Gerber baby food.
- Get BabyCenter's free email newsletter, which allows you to track your baby's development week by week and includes articles on important topics hand-picked for your particular stage of pregnancy. You'll also receive valuable coupons, sale notices, and free offers from BabyCenter and their partners. It's available at MySavings.com/offer/baby-center.asp.

Medical Insurance for Kids

Every state in the nation has a health insurance program for children under 18 years old. It's available for children in working families, and provides (at little or no cost) insurance to pay for doctor's visits, prescriptions, and much more. To see if you qualify go to InsureKidsNow.gov, then click on "Your state's program" or call 1-8777-KIDS-NOW.

Teeth Cleaning

Did you know that the first Friday in February each year is Give Kids a Smile Day? Dentists around the country provide free check-ups and cleanings to kids on this day, so if you schedule your kids' 6-month check-ups in February and August, that's one less cleaning you have to pay for! Visit the American Dental Association's website at GiveKidsASmile.ADA.org for more information.

Birthday Gifts

When you join Geoffrey's Birthday Club at Toys "R" Us, your children will get a free birthday card and gift each year until they turn 10. Check out Birthdaysrus.com/grownups for details.

Kids' Clothes

Get gently worn clothes for your kids at ThredUp.com. Through this unique online community, browse boxes of clothes that parents have put together by gender, size, season, and more. Pay $15.95 to get the entire box, then post a box of your own to share.

Lego Magazine

Calling all kids (and kids-at heart)! Lego is offering free subscriptions to their magazines. US residents can either call 1-866-534-6258 or go to Club1.lego.com/en-US/subscription/Default.aspx. They're offering two magazines: one for those under six, and one for bigger kids and adults. The subscriptions expire after two years, but you can resubscribe for free. (Canadian readers, please call 1-877-518-5346 to take advantage of this offer.)

Coloring and Activity Pages

Get free, downloadable computer games as well as coloring and activity pages for kids at PrimaryGames.com. Make sure to check out their "Holiday" section, where you can find free activities that revolve around Christmas, Halloween, Thanksgiving—even Martin Luther King, Jr. Day!

Resources for Kids

Whether you homeschool your children or one of them has expressed interest in a particular subject, it's hard to know where to turn online for accurate information. At Free.Ed.gov, you can find free, professional learning resources—including online videos, audio lectures, interactive features, and printable lessons—from government agencies. They list information by subject, including Math, Famous People, The Arts, State History, and more.

Meals for Kids

Many restaurants offer free meals for kids on particular days each week. To find a bunch in your area, visit KidsMealDeals.com. Enter your zip code and you'll find deals from chain restaurants and local joints alike, and they even have apps for iPhones and Blackberrys in case you need it on-the-go.

Keep the Kids Entertained

At FreeStuff4Kids.net, self-avowed "cheapskate mom" Randa Clay gathers all sorts of things for kids online. Some links are to cool, interactive sites that your child will enjoy, some are to online giveaways of kid-related products, and others will give you free printable worksheets and games for kids. And to never have to buy a coloring book again, head over to Free-Coloring-Pages. com, where you can find printable images for kids to color, including those of popular cartoon characters.

Yes, There is Such a Thing as a Free Lunch...

...or dinner. Kids eat free at Denny's every Tuesday night (and some Saturdays) with a paying adult. IHOP, Golden Corral, Marie Callender's, and Chevys restaurants also offer kids-eat-free deals at select locations. Just go to their websites or KidsMealDeals. com for details.

Let's Go to the Circus!

According to Ringling Bros. and Barnum & Bailey, "Parenthood brings many wonderful firsts—your baby's first tooth, your baby's first steps...and of course, your baby's first circus!" If you have a child who is under one year of age, sign up to get a free circus ticket that never expires! Just go to Ringling.com and click on "Special offers," where you'll find the "Baby's first circus" offer as well as other discount promotions.

Perks for Moms and Other Caregivers

By signing up with Amazon Mom, you'll not only get discounts on diapers and other baby supplies, you'll get a free Amazon Prime membership, which usually costs $79 and gives you free two-day shipping on every single order you place on Amazon. To sign up, just visit Amazon.com/mom. If you're a student, you can also sign up for a free Amazon Prime membership by going to Amazon.com/student.

Puppy Instruction Manual

Do you wish your puppy came with an instruction manual? Well, the folks at Pedigree have written a puppy guide that's available as a free download on Pedigree.com. Click on "Puppy Place" to find a link to the guide. There are other great deals on the Pedigree site, like $2-off coupons and more.

Pet Safety

Get a free pet safety kit at BarkBuckleUp.com. The kit will give you customized pet safety materials for your car, like a first-responders decal and emergency contact info in case your pet is harmed. You'll also receive a newsletter that gives you free pet safety advice and coupons.

Pet Food

Get a free, all-natural sample of dry food for your cat or dog at HighestQualityPetFood.com.

More All-Natural Cat or Dog Food

To get a free coupon for $3 off a bag of cat or dog food, visit BlueBuffalo.com and click on "Compare Your Brand" to find out how your brand stacks up with Blue Buffalo (hint: It doesn't have "Life Source bits") and get a free coupon.

Dog Treats

To get a free sample of Natural Nibbles dog treats, go to NaturalNibbles.com/free_samples.html. Enter your name and address, and they'll send you some of their all-natural yummies for your favorite pet!

FREE TRANSPORTATION AND FREE FOR YOUR CAR

Shuttle Transport

Once you start looking for them on the road, you'll see them everywhere. No, not bad drivers—free shuttle buses. These buses run from hotels to airports, malls to Main Street, and even sometimes to large, big-box stores like IKEA. They usually keep a regular schedule (driving in a loop) and are often mostly empty. If you're going somewhere close to a shuttle bus, why not score a ride for free? Most shuttle bus providers don't mind you hopping aboard even if you're not going to or coming from their exact destination, but it's not a bad idea to check, especially at hotels. (Some hotels will let your ride for a price.) You may find it's one of the cheapest ways to get to the airport—or to your friend's house, next to the mall.

Transportation for Seniors

Many cities and towns (including our nation's largest, New York City) offer free or discounted door-to-door transportation for senior citizens. Find out if your town offers such a service by calling your city hall or community center, or call the National

Transit Hotline at 1-800-527-8279 for a list of local transportation companies that receive money from the government to offer discounted services for seniors.

Free Car!

Go to TheFreeCar.com to get a free car! It's not that easy, of course (or that free). You have to pay a membership fee ($30 for a year), and then you will be listed in a database that is accessed by companies that are looking to give away free cars with advertisements on them in exchange for you driving the car down city streets. Your chances of being selected are way higher if you live in a more densely populated area, of course, and you'll be required to drive around town a certain number of hours per week. But hey, free car!

Protect Your Paint Job

If you're not using some of our car-care hints to clean your car, head over to ArmorAll.com. They usually have a freebie for cleaning your car on offer, like a rebate on car wax.

Tune-Ups

Join Pep Boys' auto rewards program, and you'll not only receive points with every purchase towards special offers, you'll also receive free tire rotation and flat repair, free evaluations if your check engine light goes on or you think your brakes need work, and a $20 discount on towing. You'll also receive other special offers, including coupons on your birthday. To join, just visit a Pep Boys store. (Go to PepBoys.com to find the one nearest you.)

Free Gas Prices

Before you go to the gas station, visit GasBuddy.com. Enter your zip code, and your new buddy will tell you the gas stations with the cheapest prices nearby. You can also search to find the least expensive pump prices in your entire state or entire city. You will never again fill up only to see a cheaper station on the way home!

Car How-To

If you've ever wished you knew how to diagnose problems with your car, or exactly what to ask your mechanic when you go in for a tune up, then this free book is for you. The Car Care Council offers free printed and e versions of their *Car Care Manual*, an invaluable and straightforward resource for car owners, at CarCare.org/car-care-guide.

Car Parts

According to the National Highway Traffic Safety Administration, approximately 175 car parts are recalled each year. If you're having a problem with your car, make sure to check out SaferCar. gov before you take it into the shop. The site allows you to search for recalls by part (just select "Vehicle owners" and then "Safety recalls"), which you should be able to get from a dealership for free. You can also sign up to receive email alerts about recalls for your car, and for child safety seats.

Free Medicine and Health Supplies

Freebies from Doctors

If you've just been prescribed a medication, or your doctor has suggested you take something over-the-counter, ask him if he has any free samples he could give you. Doctors are often given samples by sales reps, and don't think to hand them out until they're asked. Many pediatricians will also have free samples of baby formula available.

Free OTC Medicine

For free samples of over-the-counter medication such as Imodium, ThermaCare, and Dr. Scholl's, sign up at Register.RemedyLife.com. You'll also receive a free subscription to *Remedy* magazine.

Prescription Medicine

If you don't have a prescription plan, or if your prescription plan has denied you coverage for an expensive medication, you may be able to get it for free or at a deep discount. NeedyMeds. com will tell you how to get the medicine you need from the government, private outreach programs, and even the pharmaceutical companies themselves. Just simply find the name of your medication in the "Brand name" or "Generics" list and see if you qualify! You should never be without the prescriptions you need.

Free Relief

If you or someone in your family is lactose intolerant, you know how hard it can be to get necessary calcium. To try a free sample of Lactaid lactose-free milk, go to Lactaid.com/content/offer-page.

Free from Heartburn

If you frequently suffer from heartburn, you may qualify for a free sample of Prilosec OTC heartburn medication. Just go to PrilosecOTC.TrustedForm.com and fill out the quick form to see if you're eligible.

Vitamins

Naturemade Vitamins has a Wellness Rewards program that allows you to accumulate points when you purchase their products and use the points for vitamin coupons, exercise DVDs, and more. Visit their website at Naturemade.com and click on "Wellness Rewards." The "Coupon Center" link on the same page directs you to other great offers.

Get Your Omega-3s!

Omega-3 fatty acids are an essential dietary supplement that promote a healthy heart, brain, eyes, and joints. Get a free, printable, $5-off coupon for Coromega, an Omega-3 supplement, at Coromega.com/free-sample.

Contact Lenses

If you have a prescription for contacts, you can get a certificate for a free pair of Acuvue disposable lenses, at Acuvue.com. Just click on the "Free lenses" link.

Health Care

The Health Resources and Services Administration (HRSA.gov) can direct you to a health center that provides health and dental care to people of all ages, whether or not they have health insurance or a lot of money. Just go to their site, enter your ZIP code, and click on "Find Centers."

Kick the Habit

Trying to quit smoking? You're on the way to savings already. But did you know that you can often obtain smoking cessation products such as nicotine gum and patches for free? Many states and cities offer free products or reimbursements, especially if you are on a fixed income. Also check with your employer, school, or health insurance company to see if they offer free products. Finally, head over to Nicoderm CQ's website (NicodermCQ.com) for a free patch and a coupon for their product. If that's not enough, think about how much you'll save when you don't have to buy cigarettes anymore!

Begin the Journey to a Healthier Life

Trends in dieting seem to change with the season. One day you're being told to eat plain toast, the next, bacon—it all gets a little confusing! That's where FatSecret.com comes in. Create a personalized exercise and nutrition program, then share it with their online community for moral support and feedback. Plus, you can track your progress, keep an online fitness journal, and research different diets and fitness techniques. Another fitness site we love is MyHomePersonalTrainer.com, where you can calculate your ideal weight and heart rate, assess your cardiovascular fitness, and receive all sorts of free advice to help you start getting in shape.

Just as Good as Weight Watchers

If you're like most of us, your New Year's resolution includes something about losing weight. Get a free, online journal to track

how many calories you consume and burn at My-Calorie-Counter.
com. Search for the food you're eating by restaurant or type, and
enter what kind of exercise you're doing and for how long. The
site will help you stay on track to success.

Exercise Videos

Don't pay for aerobics, yoga, pilates, and other exercise videos!
Instead, head over to ExerciseTV.tv, where you can find a wide
variety of free, professional exercise videos. If you have a cable
box, you may also have access to Exercise TV free on-demand!
Just check your On Demand or channel listings.

Diabetes Meter

You can get a portable diabetes meter, absolutely free, at Meter.
DiabeticConnect.com. It's a One Touch "UltraMini," and you can
pick the color of your choice.

FREE FINANCIAL TOOLS

Free Checking, with Interest

At ING Direct, you never have to wait in line to see a teller—
because they have no physical locations! Of course, if you're
like us, you can't remember the last time you actually saw a teller
anyway. The great thing about ING is that they not only offer
free savings and CD accounts, but you can get an absolutely
fee-free checking account that also gives you up to 1.24 percent
interest! They'll also send you a debit card and checks, and you
get free access to All-Point Network ATMs, which can be found
in many drugstores and convenience stores. To put money into
the account, set up direct deposit with your employer, or transfer

money from other bank accounts for free. Visit INGDirect.com for more information and to open an account.

Free ATMs

Sick of paying up to $3 every time you have to visit an ATM? At AllPointNetwork.com, you can find all of the surcharge-free ATMs in your area by entering your city and state or your zip code. Many of the listings are for stores that offer cash-back with purchase, but you never know when you'll find a free ATM you never knew about.

Check for Free Checks

The next time you're coming to the end of your box of checks, don't pay the bank for more. Instead, go to StylesChecks.com, where you can get a second box of checks for only 49 cents when you purchase your first box (just look for the link that says "pricing" to see the special introductory offer). Also visit ChecksUnlimited.com/Introoffer.aspx, where you can get a free box of checks when you order three more boxes.

Free Accounting Help

We know how hard it can be to deal with money stress. But if you go to Wesabe.com, you can get free tools and advice on how to take control of your finances. You can see all your bank and credit card balances in one place and learn ways to get ahead in just a few easy steps. It's worth a try!

Online Financial Planning

Is there anything the internet can't do? Now you can create a personalized picture of your finances without shelling out thousands of dollars for a session with an adviser. Kiplinger.com is our favorite site to help you get on the right financial track. Hunt around their site to find treasure troves of free financial advice. Then head over to Voyant (PlanWithVoyant.com) to map your financial goals (such as buying a home, saving for retirement, or paying for your kids' college) along an interactive timeline. It's a great way to plan for the future and chart your progress.

Free Budgeting Templates

Keeping track of your budget is important not only in helping you save, but in identifying bad spending habits that you can easily fix. Get free budget trackers to use in Microsoft Excel by visiting Vertex42.com and clicking on "Excel templates."

—Greg Chu, Fayetteville, NC

Credit Score

Did you know that legally, you are entitled to one free credit report per year? However, many credit report sites will make you pay to see your score, or charge you a membership or "credit monitoring" fee. Visit CreditKarma.com for a free, no-strings-attached estimation of your credit score. Then go to AnnualCreditReport.com to see how they came up with that score, and to make sure there are no errors on your report.

Tax Preparation

Get your federal taxes filed for free! Turbo Tax is offering a free copy of their easy-to-use tax preparation software to anyone who made less than $31,000 last year, or was in active duty military and had an adjusted gross income of less than $58,000. Just go to Turbotax.Intuit.com/taxfreedom to get started. If you live in one of the following states, you can also use their software to file your state taxes for free: Alabama, Arkansas, Arizona, Georgia, Iowa,

Idaho, Kentucky, Michigan, Minnesota, Mississippi, Montana, New York, North Carolina, North Dakota, Okalahoma, Oregon, Rhode Island, South Carolina, Vermont or West Virginia.

More Help Filing Your Taxes

The IRS free-filing service provides free federal income tax return preparation and electronic filing for all taxpayers. All you need is access to a computer and the Internet and you can prepare and e-file your federal tax return for free! Free file offers two options. The first, called Free File, is for filers whose incomes are $57,000 per year or less. Free File allows you to prepare your taxes using one of the 20 tax preparation software products on their site. If you make more than $57,000, the IRS has decided you can afford to pay for these programs yourself! But you can still use their Free File Fillable Forms, which are electronic versions of the usual paper forms that you can file online for free. To access either service, go to www.IRS.gov/freefile.

Help for Your Home

If you're having money problems and are worried about losing your home, help is on the way. Go to NFCC.org/housing/orderdvd.cfm to get a free DVD on how to avoid foreclosure from the National Foundation for Credit Counseling.

FREE CLASSES AND HOW-TO

Learn to Cook

Love to cook or wish you knew more? Take free cooking classes at your local Williams-Sonoma store. They offer technique classes and product demonstrations that range from making your own soda to cooking steak to dinner-worthy sandwiches. To locate your nearest Williams-Sonoma and to see their events calendar, go to Williams-Sonoma.com and click on "Store locator." Then keep an eye out for the "Store events" section.

Crafty Classes

Did you know that, in addition to selling craft supplies at great prices, Michael's also offers free classes on making crafts? Free classes often center around a holiday (such as Mother's Day, Fourth of July, or Thanksgiving), and will teach you how to make something you can bring home as a present or decoration. Michael's also offers more general classes on beading, painting, and other crafts for a small fee or free with purchase. To find out what your local Michael's is offering, go to Michaels.com and click on "Find a store." Once you've located your nearest Michael's, click on "This store's events" to see what kind of crafts you can learn for free.

For Do-It-Yourself Kids

At The Home Depot's Kids Workshops, you and your child can build fun projects like toolboxes, fire trucks, mail organizers, birdhouses, and bug containers. The workshops are free, designed for kids 5–12, and occur the first Saturday of each month in all Home Depot stores. These fantastic classes not only give you a fun activity to share with your kid (adult participation is required), they teach safety and skills. In addition to the newly constructed project, each child receives a kid-sized Home Depot apron and an achievement pin. Details can be found at HomeDepot.com. Once there, just enter "Kids workshops" in their search bar.

Lowe's How-To Clinics for Kids

Lowe's is another good source for DIY kids' projects. Bring the entire brood into any Lowe's store and build a free wooden project. Each participant also receives a free apron, goggles, a project-themed patch, and a certification of merit upon completion of the project. Clinics are offered every other Saturday from 10 a.m. to 11 a.m., and all building materials and tools are provided. Get the details at LowesBuildAndGrow.com.

Language Lessons

Take lessons in Spanish, French, Italian, and German absolutely free at BBC.co.uk/languages and you can travel internationally more easily (or just impress your friends). The site also offers quickie lessons in Chinese, Japanese, and even more exotic languages like Kudu.

Live to Learn

At GCFLearnFree.org, you can finally learn how to use all those computer programs that have been befuddling you. Sign up for classes taught over the internet, or download learning materials to go at your own pace. Classes include Microsoft Windows, Word, and Excel, internet searching, and email basics. The site also offers free lessons in managing money, math skills, and "everyday life" problems.

Computer Lessons

If you own a Mac product or are thinking of buying one, you should know that there are free classes available to you at your local Apple store. Whether you're trying to figure out how to use your new iPhone or want to learn how to easily make a website for your business, you can sign up for free course that will teach you how. Their most useful class, however, might be for beginning computer users. Perfect for seniors, it will teach you how to set up a printer, hook your computer up to email, and other computer basics. For more information, ask at an Apple store or visit Apple.com/retail/workshops.

Tech Support

It turns out that membership to Sam's Club gives you a lot more than bargain prices! Even if you didn't buy your computer, TV, or other electronic from Sam's Club, you can still call their 24-hour tech support for help at 877-758-4346. Costco will also help members with tech problems, as long as the item was purchased at their store. Give them at call at 866-861-0450.

Business Skills

The US Small Business Association is dedicated to helping your small business succeed. At their site, SBA.gov, you'll not only find free tools and resources for small business owners, but free classes as well! These online courses are each about 30 minutes long and will teach you about financing your business, marketing and advertising, obtaining government contracts, and more. Just go to SBA.gov and click on "Counseling and Training."

Career Advice

Get all kinds of free, professional advice on your career (or desired career) at CareerOneStop.com (or call 1-877-348-0502), which will give you tutorials on résumés and cover letters, give you salary information, help you find free classes in your area, and more. If you're working on your résumé, check out ResumeCompanion.com. Indicate what position you're applying for, and it will give you the perfect phrases to describe the type of work you've done at previous employers.

College without Tuition

Believe it or not, there is such a thing as a free college! Of course, they're so few and far between that these schools are pretty hard to get into, but if you or your teen is looking at competitive universities, these should go at the top of the list! College of the Ozarks in Missouri, Berea College in Kentucky, and the Cooper Union and the Webb Institute in New York are all 100 percent tuition-free. Many military colleges also have not only free tuition, but free room and board. They include the Coast Guard Academy in Connecticut, Air Force Academy in Colorado, Naval Academy in Maryland, and Merchant Marine Academy and West Point in New York.

First-Class Education

Massachusetts Institute of Technology—one of the United States' most preeminent technological universities—offers free course materials online. Get reading lists, homework assignments, and audio and/or video lectures for a mind-boggling variety of classes including SCUBA diving, written language for Chinese speakers, TV theory, and 1,895 more. Want to really impress your friends? Try some classes on calculus, brain structure, bioengineering, even "Wheelchair Design in Developing Countries." If you're willing to put in the time to learn, these classes will definitely teach you things you never knew. Visit the site at OCW.MIT.edu to get started.

Study Guides and Test Prep for Students

Don't pay for those little bright yellow books! You can now read Cliffs Notes free online just by going to CliffsNotes.com. Also check out SparkNotes.com, which has free study guides for hundreds of books as well as free test prep for the SAT, ACT, and more.

Civil Service Test Prep

If you're applying for a government job, you probably need to take a civil service exam. But don't spend money on expensive test prep books or software. Instead, go to PSE-net.com/library. htm. This site, run by the Public Service Employees Network, gives you links to buy books about each of the exams, but also provides links to free resources offered by various states and other organizations. Just click on the type of test you will be taking, and see what they have on offer.

Informative Brochures

You can get a book or pamphlet on virtually any subject, free of charge, by logging onto Pueblo.GSA.gov or calling 1-888-878-3256. The Federal Citizen Information Center offers free publications on cars, employment, housing, travel, money—the list goes on. Sometimes there is a small fee for shipping and handling; in all cases, you can download the text for free. You never know what you might find here! Whether or not you find what you're looking for, it's always an interesting site to check out.

How Do I...?

To learn how to do just about anything, visit WonderHowTo.com, which culls instructional videos from more than 1,700 websites. You can check out what's hot, do a custom search, or browse through such categories as family, electronics, software, dance, fitness, magic tricks, and pets. Whether you want to learn how to cut your own hair, use Photoshop software, or make a shot glass out of ice, you'll find it here.

FREE FOR YOUR OFFICE

Finally Get that Pen Refill!

Gather up those fancy pens with the empty ink cartridges in them and head over to FreeRefill.com for free ink refills. You'll have to pay a shipping fee, but they offer free refills for 17 different models of pens.

Computer Help

For something called "Help," that particular menu item on any computer program is unbelievably unhelpful! The next time you find yourself throwing your hands up in frustration in front of the computer, head over to ProTonic.com. Type in a question, and get a free, prompt email response from a volunteer computer expert. Who needs an IT department?

Free File Conversion

Converting electronic documents into PDF files usually requires buying expensive software. But at PrimoPDF.com/online.aspx, you can convert any printable document (like Word documents, images, and PowerPoint presentations) into a PDF online for free. You can also download free software for your PC that will do the same thing on your desktop.

Why Pay for Microsoft?

"Great Software…Easy to Use…and it's Free!" That's the claim at OpenOffice.org, and it's true. Check out their free word processing and spreadsheet programs that are similar to programs that Microsoft offers. Another good site for these types of programs is Google Docs: Docs.Google.com. At Google Docs you can open Microsoft Word and other files, then share them over the internet with others.

The Best Software, Absolutely Free

The best price for new software? How about free?! GiveawayOfTheDay.com offers brand new software absolutely free—you'll never be prompted to register for the "full" version, and the software will never expire. The catch is that each program is usually only offered for 24 hours, so make sure to act fast! Subscribe to Giveaway of the Day's email newsletter and they'll let you know which software packages are going to be offered in the upcoming week. You can also follow them on Facebook and Twitter.

More Free Software

At Download.com, you can download free screensavers, anti-virus software, games, and more. Just type what you're looking for in their search bar, then click "Free" under "Narrow Your Search" on the left.

A Super Hero for Your Computer

Windows Defender is software that helps protect your computer against pop-ups, slow performance, and security threats caused by spyware and other unwanted software by detecting it and removing it from your computer. Windows Defender features

"Real-Time Protection," a monitoring system that recommends actions against spyware when it's detected, minimizes interruptions, and helps you stay productive. It's free if you own Windows. Just go to Microsoft.com and search for "defender."
—*Karen Matsu Greenberg, New York, NY*

Virus Got you Down?

That's a computer virus we're talking about, of course. For free anti-virus protection, head to Free.AVG.com.

Before Your Computer Crashes

Did you know that nearly one in four computer users have lost content to blackouts, viruses, and hackers? Fortunately, you can protect your important files and photos from computer crashes, theft, or natural disasters, absolutely free. At Dropbox.com, get 2 gigabytes of free and secure digital storage space. MyOtherDrive.com offers a similar deal as well.

File Too Large to Email?

Most email servers choke on attachments that are 10 megabytes or larger, but you can avoid that problem with Box.net. Upload files of up to 25 megabytes, then receive a customizable web address that you can send to your contacts so they can download the files. You get up to 5 gigabytes of free storage. Users can even leave notes and collaborate in other ways right on the site.

Free Faxes

Never pay for a fax again! Instead, go to FaxZero.com, where they'll let you either enter text to be faxed or upload a PDF or Word document. Pay a $2 fee and they won't put their ad on the cover page.

Free Wireless Internet

Tons of coffee shops, book stores, hotels, and public buildings offer wireless internet service for free or free-with-purchase. Find local "hot spots" at WiFiFreeSpot.com, and don't forget to submit any WiFi zones you find for others on-the-go.

FREE FOR YOUR PHONE

Everything for Your Mobile

At Cell11.com, find freebies for your cell phone, from wallpapers to software to ringtones to games. Just select what kind of phone you have, and the site will tell you what free stuff is available. You can also try CellBits.com.

Make Your Own Ringtones

Ever wished you create a ringtone of your favorite song? Well now you can at IWFR.net/mp3toringtone. Upload an MP3 file and the site will convert it to a file that your phone can use as a ringtone.

Free Ringtones from An Unlikely Source

If you'd like a new ringtone for your phone that's just a simple melody, download some surprisingly sweet ditties at Friskies.com (yes, the cat food brand). Just go to Friskies.com/Downloads and enter your phone number, and they'll send the ringtone right to your phone for free.

To-Do Lists Made Easy

We absolutely adore Remember the Milk, a task organizer that goes far beyond your web browser. Even if you don't have a fancy phone, you can add things to your online calendar and get reminders from your cell phone! It also allows you to easily share lists and calendars (like with your spouse), and map your appointments before you go. To find out more and download for free, go to RememberTheMilk.com.

Phone Calls

Make free phone calls to practically anywhere in the world with Skype—software you download, then use to talk to people through your computer speakers and microphone. You can also call cell phones and land lines for as low as 2¢ a minute. Visit Skype.com to start chatting.

Free 411

Never pay an outrageous fee for 411 services again. Just call the AT&T Yellow Pages at 1-800-935-5697. You'll have to listen to a quick, pre-taped commercial, but you won't pay anything beyond your normal airtime minutes.

Cell Phone Plan

If you receive government assistance in any form, you may be eligible for a free cell phone and 250 minutes of talk time per month. Just visit SafeLinkWireless.com or AssuranceWirless.com to see if you qualify, find out if your state offers the program, and to apply. You'll also receive free voicemail and text messaging!

Free Info Via Text Message

Google isn't just for the internet anymore. Now if you need information on-the-go you can text Google with your cell phone. This is especially useful for addresses and phone numbers. Simply type in the business name and your city or zip code and text to 466-45 (G-O-O-G-L). This service is also great for settling bets: Type in "Mt. Everest elevation" and get the answer instantly. Or text "weather" and your zip code to get a three-day forecast. Normal text-messaging rates for your plan apply, but you won't be charged any extra.

Better Than Tying a String Around Your Finger

Never forget the important stuff again with TextReminder.net. They offer free reminders by allowing you to enter text, then sending it as a text message to your cell phone at the time you specify. You can even schedule a daily, weekly, monthly, or yearly text reminder. SMS charges apply.

More Free Apps

FreeAppADay.com is our favorite site for free apps! They offer apps for iPhone, iPad, and Android that normally cost up to $4, but are being offered for a limited time for promotional purposes. Apps that are being offered change daily, so make sure to sign up for their email alerts or follow them on Facebook or Twitter!

Stop Paying for Texts!

TxtDrop.com enables users in the United States and Canada to send text messages with instant delivery, absolutely free. No more needing to pay your cellular provider for sending your friend a text. (Many plans charge up to 25¢ a pop!) Just enter your email address (for replies), your friend's mobile number, and your message, and they'll send your text instantly, completely free of charge.

Even More Free and Easy Texts

Did you know that just about every phone plan allows you to receive texts by email? To use your (or your friends') phone's email address, just type the phone number in the "to" field of your email and follow the @ sign with the following addresses: txt.att.net for AT&T customers, vtext.com for Verizon customers, tmomail.net for T-Mobile, messaging.sprintpcs.com for Sprint, message.alltell.com for Alltel, and vmobl.com for Virgin. Just be aware that because your email address pops up, you can't always use the full 160 characters! Or get the phone's email address by sending yourself an email from it—just write a text message and enter your email address where you'd normally type the phone number.

FREE HOBBY AND CRAFT SUPPLIES

Digital Srapbooking

Digital scrapbooking has many benefits over "regular" scrapbooking—you can easily redo everything, you don't have to worry about cutting or writing in a straight line—and once you buy the software, it's free! Whether you've never tried digital scrapbooking or you're an old pro, check out ShabbyPrincess. com for free downloads of various scrapbooking themes, plus free video tutorials that will show you how to use the themes and get started on making your own digital scrapbooks. Just visit ShabbyPrincess.com and click on either "Tutorials" or "Downloads" at the top.

Photo Sharing

Store your cherished digital photos and videos for free at Photobucket.com, Flickr.com, and Picasa.com. These sites not only provide a back-up in case the files on your computer get lost, they also allow you to easily share photos with friends. You can also keep your photos on sites where you order photos, such as Walmart.com, Snapfish.com, and Shutterfly.com. Be aware, however, that these sites only allow you to store photos as long as your account is active.

Patterns

Get free patterns from the leader in sewing—Butterick/McCall. Just go to Butterick.McCall.com and click on "Free project" or go directly to Butterick.McCall.com/free-downloads-pages-1013.php. Sign up for their email program and get access to a wide variety of free patterns, most of which are for crafts.

More Sewing Patterns

Get free patterns for sewing, quilting, knitting, crocheting, and even paper crafts at FreePatterns.com. Just download and print out!

Free for Knitters and Crocheters

Grab your needles or hook and get ready for some new things to knit or crochet! Check out KnittingPatternCentral.com/directory.php for free knitting patterns of all sorts, including afghans, rugs, garments, toys, and just about anything you can think of. (Try CrochetPatternCentral.com for crochet patterns.) The Lion brand yarn company also offers free patterns if you join their site—just visit LionBrand.com/patterns. Other great sites for free knitting and crocheting patterns are FreeVintageKnitting.com and KnittingOnTheNet.com.

For the Cross-Stitcher

Like to cross-stitch? Never pay for a cross-stitching pattern again! Get access to hundreds of free cross-stitching projects at Dawn's Cross Stitch. Just go to DawnsXstitch.PWP.Blueyonder.co.uk and click on "Alphabetical list of patterns" or "Patterns by category."

Stickers

If you have a kid who loves to collect stickers, you know that they'll save practically anything with a self-adhesive backing. For an extensive list of free stickers available online, Freaky Freddie is your go-to guy! Just visit FreakyFreddies.com/sticker.htm. They also list bumper stickers, in case it's time to plaster over that one from the 2000 election.

Calendars and Other Printables

They might not be as great as our Who Knew? calendars, but you can get a free calendar by visiting PrintFree.com. Select from a number of different styles, then customize with any important dates you'd like to add, and print! The site also offers free printable signs and cards.

FREE GAMES

For the Puzzle Lover

In the mood for a puzzle? Head over to Puzzles.About.com and click on "Free puzzles." You'll find a wide array of puzzles you can play online, including crosswords, sudoku, word searches, and even online jigsaw puzzles!

Fun, Brought to You by the Letters PBS

Need to keep young kids busy for a few valuable minutes? Head to PBS.org/sesame for a variety of free *Sesame Street*–themed games. You can also print out coloring pages, bookmarks, and other kids' activities. Best of all, you can search via character, so you can find activities based around your child's *Sesame Street* favorites.

Play Your Favorite Card Games Online

Has the boss disabled your solitaire game at work? Try out IdiotsDelight.net, where you can choose from more than two dozen solitaire card games you can play online. Click on "Klondike" to play "regular" solitaire. Warning: you might get hooked!

Brain Games

Need even more free stuff to keep the kids busy? At LightUpYourBrain.com, you'll find free games for kids, as well as downloadable audio books of children's stories.

More Online Games

If you're looking for games for the kids—or an excuse to act like a kid yourself—head to Kongregate.com, which boasts more than 24,000 free games. There are tons of free games at Pogo.com and OnlineFlashGames.org as well.

Chess Lessons

When our oldest son asked us how to play chess, we knew this was a parenting challenge we weren't up to. So we headed over to ChessKids.com, which gave us free lessons, quizzes, and games to teach our son chess. It also allows you to play chess against a computer, and offers resources for people wanting to start a chess club at their school.

Board Games

Step away from the computer! Well, after you print out some free board games, that is. Check out Interformic.com for original, imaginative games that you can print and play. For free games that use items you already have on-hand like cards and dice, check out Invisible-City.com/play.

Road Trip Entertainment

Never have to worry about what your kids are going to do in the car again with Rad Roadtrips. At their site, you can download free activity books for kids especially designed to keep them entertained in the car. The site also has individual coloring pages and a maze generator. Just go to RadRoadtrips.com and click on "Downloads."

Free Movies, Music, Books, and More

A Night at the Movies

These days, it costs a small fortune to take your family to the movies. But at FilmMetro.com, you can get free tickets to advanced screenings and movies that have just been released! Search by city, or browse current listings. The pickings here are often slim, but the site gives you a sneak peak at future offerings, so if you make it a habit to check back often, you may be able to snag free tickets to the latest blockbuster.

Free Rentals

At Redbox, renting movies couldn't be easier. Just keep an eye out for their big red boxes at stores near you. To get a free rental your first time, go to Redbox.com/movienight.

Where The Wild Files Are: Finding Free Music Online

Pretty much any computer these days comes with some kind of program to play MP3s, and other music files, and MP3s files are easy to find on the internet. You should be aware, though, that many sites that offer free MP3s aren't legal, as there are laws in place to make sure that studios and artists get money for their songs. Here are some sites, however, where you can find free, legal MP3 files to download.

- Amazon.com offers dozens of free MP3s as special promotions. To find them, simply select "MP3 downloads" from the drop-down search menu. When the list pops up, select "Price: low to high" from the drop-down sort menu on the upper right-hand side of the MP3 list. You can also subscribe to an email newsletter that keeps you apprised of new deals—keep an eye out for the "Amazon delivers" ad on the left side of the screen and click on "subscribe now."

- If you're a fan of old radio shows like *Amos & Andy*, Bing Crosby specials, and the *Benny Goodman Show*, check out RadioLovers.com, which gives you free downloads of hundreds of classic programs.
- If you use iTunes, check the iTunes store regularly for free tracks, which you can easily find on the main page or the music home page.
- EMusic.com offers 40 free music downloads as an incentive to get you to join their site, which has more than 13 million offerings. Most downloads start at just 49¢ each, and you'll get a $20 credit just for joining. (Note: eMusic sometimes changes this offer, so act fast!)
- For easy-to-download MP3s of all varieties, go to Sideload. com, which pulls MP3s from free sources from around the internet.

You Don't Need Cable to Watch *The Daily Show*

If you have a fast internet connection and a fairly new computer, you can watch TV and movies online for free! At Hulu.com, you can watch TV right on your monitor. Play the most recent episodes of shows from FOX, NBC, Comedy Central, and other networks; or classics like *The Dick Van Dyke Show* and *Alfred Hitchcock Presents*. They even have a good selection of movies, whether you're looking for something to entertain the kids or something R-rated for date night.

More Movies and TV

If you're looking for free movies and TV shows online, head over to SlashControl.com. They have more than 84,000 free videos, including some great family movies and TV shows old and new.

Free Online Movies

At Crackle.com, you can find hundreds of free movies to watch online. They have an especially good collection of horror movies and comedy flicks, including lots of Monty Python. Also included are a few TV shows.

Online Magazines

If you don't mind reading magazines on the computer (or printing them out), you can get them for free. Head over to Zinio. com, where you can download a free "digital" issue of many magazines, including *Reader's Digest, Hello!,* and *Women's Health.*

Books

No one likes to throw away a book. Therefore, it's easy to find places that give away books or offer them for a dollar or less. Check with your community's recycling center to see if they offer free books that people have thrown in their bin, and ask your local library if they ever have book sales. Online, go to PaperbackSwap.com. Featured on the *Today Show* and in *Real Simple* and *Good Housekeeping,* the site allows you list books (not just paperbacks) you don't want any more. Once you send them to other users, you'll get credits you can use toward a new (to you) book of your own.

The New Book

Download free e-books instantly at EbookPlanet.net. They have books across all categories—pets, business, finance, house & garden, computers, and even novels—all absolutely free. Other good places to find free e-books are Scridb.com, Free-Ebooks.net, and SmashWords.com.

American Classics in Your Inbox

Sign up to receive a free story every week via email at Email.LOA.org/sotw_signup_index.jsp. These free stories aren't just any stories—they're revered classics from the Library of America, a non-profit organization dedicated to publishing works by America's most treasured authors. As they say, each week's story "could be anything: a short work of fiction, a character sketch, an essay, a journalist's dispatch, a poem…. What is certain is that it will be memorable, because every story is from one of the hundreds of classic works of American literature published by The Library of America."

More Online Books

When copyrights expire, the work in question goes into the public domain. That means you can get classic books for free, and it's all perfectly legal. Check out Project Gutenberg at Gutenberg.org, where you can download more than 30,000 e-books, including works by Mark Twain, Sir Arthur Conan Doyle, Jane Austen, and other favorites. At Books.Google.com, you can search the text of even more books, including those that are still under copyright.

Free Love (Stories)!

Head over to RavenousRomance.com for a free, steamy short story each and every day! Then check out their great deals on full-length online novels. (Warning: Some of the stories are explicit!)

Sheet Music

The Mutopia Project might sound like a top-secret government plan, but the it's actually an organization that compiles sheet music that has gone into the public domain. Go to MutopiaProject.org to download sheet music for classical music by Bach, Beethoven, Chopin, Handel, Mozart, and many others.

Free Mozart

Music can be very important to a child's development, and many moms-to-be also swear by playing music for their babies before they're even born! For free downloads of classical music by Mozart that are designed especially for babies and kids, go to Munchkin.com/mozart-downloads.

Lull Yourself to Sleep

Don't spend money on a "white noise" machine to help lull you to sleep! Instead, just go to SimplyNoise.com for free streaming audio. If you want to download a file, they require a donation of at least $1. They have an hour-long thunderstorm, as well as loopable files of white, "pink," and "brown" noise. Sweet dreams!

More Free Radio

Last.fm is more than just a free radio station—it's a music-listening experience that's personalized just for you. Select your favorite songs and artists, and Last.fm will play other songs that are similar.

It's a great way to discover new bands—and it's even better than satellite radio.

Free Laughs

Get free jokes at E-Jokes.net. They list jokes by categories, like birthdays, Christmas, animals, and more. For funny videos, check out CollegeHumor.com and FunnyOrDie.com.

A BIT OF EVERYTHING

Visit WhoKnewTips.com!

We don't mind doing a bit of shameless self-promotion for our site, WhoKnewTips.com, because we know you're sure to find some great freebies and money-saving ideas when you visit. In addition to listing the most recent freebies and discounts we've found around the web, you can submit your own tips to be featured in our next book and find out more about Who Knew? products and Bruce's latest appearances on HSN. You can also follow us on Facebook and Twitter by going to Facebook.com/whoknewtips or Twitter.com/whoknewtips.

Online Dating Without the Fees

One in five people meet their mate online, but if you're interested in online dating don't pay for sites like eHarmony or Match.com. We've known just as many couples who have met on OKCupid. com—a great, free site that allows you to set up a profile and take compatibility quizzes to meet other singles in your area. Unlike other "free" dating sites, they don't try to get you to pay to have your profile listed first in search results, or for extra messaging privileges. The entire thing is free to everyone, so you're sure to at least meet someone who shares one interest with you—free stuff!

Free Tour Guide!

To get a real feel for a city when you're traveling, team up with a local from the Global Greeter Network. Visit GlobalGreeterNetwork.com to find someone who's willing to share their love of their city by showing you around—for free! By going through a city with a Global Greeter, you can experience it in a unique way, from the perspective of a person who lives there. Tours can last a couple hours or longer, the service is free, and there's a strict no-tipping policy. Cities include New York, Chicago, Paris, and Toronto.

Need a Place to Stay?

Talk about hospitality! It's not as good as having a friend with a spare room, but at CouchSurfing.org you can connect with almost 2 million members who may be willing to offer you a free place to stay while you're traveling to their city.

Painting Tool

If you've ever painted an entire room and wished you could change the color with a snap of your fingers, then this freebie is for you. Visit Behr.com and register with their site to use their "Paint Your Place" program for free. It will allow you to upload a picture of a room in your home, then change the wall color without having to buy a bucket of paint (and spend all day painting).

Proctor & Gamble Products

To get free samples of everything from body wash to laundry detergent to toothpaste, go to PGEverydaySolutions.com and click on "Register today" to get free samples of Proctor & Gamble products. You'll also receive their excellent email newsletter, which has household tips and tricks as well as a wide variety of coupons.

Savings, Right at Home

RightAtHome.com is a savings site by Johnson & Johnson. In addition to promoting their household products, they also have lots of great tips for organizing, crafts, cooking, and cleaning. The best part, of course, is their "Special offers" section, which has big coupons and free samples for products like Ziploc bags, Scrubbing Bubbles cleaner, Glade air fresheners, Windex window washing kits, Drano drain declogger, and more.

Charmin Free Offers

For coupons and freebies from Charmin toilet paper, surf on over to Charmin.com and click on the "Coupons and offers" link.

Free Clean Teeth, a Click Away

Visit Colgate.com and click on "Special offers" for coupons and free samples of toothpaste, dish soap, and other household goods.

Juicy Discounts

Don't throw away your orange juice cap or you could be throwing away savings! Register at Tropicana.com for their "Juicy Rewards" program, then look for the 10-digit code under the cap of any Tropicana product. Enter the code on the site to get points toward discounts on theme parks, outdoor gear, gym memberships, and more. The great part about this program is that you get to pick your prizes, and most of them only require a few points each.

Swagbucks

"It's like a frequent flyer mile for using the web," Swagbucks. com says about their internet rewards program. Swagbucks can be redeemed in their online store for video games, free MP3 downloads, toys, posters, office supplies, gift cards from major retailers, magazine subscriptions, and more. To earn Swagbucks, simply search the web from Search.Swagbucks.com and click on your point rewards when they pop up! You can also earn points by subscribing to their newsletter, following them on Facebook and Twitter, and taking surveys and polls. If you're interested in earning freebies easily online, this is the program for you.

Free Everything, from People Like You

You can find hundreds of items—from furniture to books to clothes to exercise equipment—at Freecycle.org, a non-profit website whose goal is to decrease landfill waste. Users join up and post about items they are giving away or need, and connect with other users who want the items or have what they're looking for. Just be careful—some free things are hard to resist, but do you really need that bedazzled couch cover?

Freebies for Getting Gifts!

Getting married? Many stores now offer freebies and rewards just for having gifts purchased on your registry! Check out Kohls.com, Macys.com, and JCPenney.com for more information.

Missing Medals

If you or a deceased family member received service medals from the army, navy, air force, marines, or other service and they have been lost, you can obtain free replacements from the US government. For more information, visit Archives.gov/veterans/replace-medals.html.

Living with Cents, and Freebies

LivingWithCents.com is a site for frugal college students. It offers great advice for saving money, but better yet, freebies! Once you're at the site, head to the "Promotions" tab. They offer a variety of goodies, and change them regularly.

Happy Birthday!

If you're not sure what to do for your birthday, how about getting something for free? If we didn't offer you enough birthday deals in this book, head over to Free Birthday Treats, an easy, one-stop resource of all things free on your birthday. Check it out at FreeBirthdayTreatsBlog.com.

Sweet Freebies

RedPlum.com is a "sweet" site for savings! They have exclusive coupons for groceries and local restaurants (lots of pizza delivery places), but we especially love their "Sweet Finds" section, which features freebies and big coupons, and can be found at RedPlum.com/pages/SweetFinds.aspx.

Free Miscellaneous

For all kinds of freebies, check out FreeFig.com. They have everything from beauty products to household cleaners to medicine. The best part is that it's updated daily, so you can check back often for the latest offers!

Thanks, Walmart!

Not only is Walmart one of the best stores to find discounts, but they also give away free samples on their website! Once you get to Walmart.com, though, they're sometimes hard to find. Look for their "In stores now" section, then click on "Free samples." They have several freebie offers each week, but you'll have to answer a short survey and may not receive the sample if you don't qualify. For example, if you're applying for a free sample of Purina One cat food, but admit you don't have cats, you may not be freebie-worthy!

How About a House Party?

What could be better than inviting all your friends over and giving them a handful of freebies? HouseParty.com lets you do just that! Their company partners with products, TV shows, and more to bring you exclusive freebies, just for throwing a party in your home. Go to HouseParty.com, pick which products interest you, and sign up to host one of the many house parties that will all take place on the same day around the US. You'll be asked to post photos of the event, send out invitations from the site, and fill out extensive surveys about your experience. But in return, you can sample a wide array of free products. Recent giveaways have included Hasbro board games, Gerber baby food, Febreeze products, and Canon photo printers. The party host or hostess also receives special gifts like decorations, gift cards, or even camcorders! The only catch is that you don't always get chosen to host the parties you sign up for. Companies are looking for outgoing, social people who will promote their products, so make sure to answer their questionnaire with that in mind! Also, be sure to check the site in the late summer, when they often list TV premiere parties that will give you access to new shows before their debut on TV!

T-Shirts (with Typos)

Want a free T-shirt? Just go to Petrix.com/Shirt. There, you'll find companies that have donated shirts that have printing errors on them. They didn't want their employees or customers to wear them—but they're yours for the taking. And hey, wearing a shirt with a typo is a great conversation starter!

CHAPTER 4

Free Stuff Strategies

No one knows who was the first person to say "the best things in life are free," but it's true whether you're talking about love and happiness or just getting a free deodorant sample in the mail. If you love freebies as much as we do, check out these easy ways to get even more samples and prizes with just a little legwork.

Browse Freebie Websites

It's easy to get product samples for free over the internet. Here are some of our favorite sites that compile free offers from other websites. We like some of these sites because they have everything, and others because they pre-screen the offers beforehand. Check them regularly and see what you find!

- StartSampling.com pulls together online offers for free samples, from everything from magazine subscriptions to vitamins. The site also offers some valuable coupons that you can print out and take with you to the store.

- One of our favorite sites for freebies is FreeSampleFreak.com. Brandie, the free sample freak from this blog's title, brings you all kind of offers from around the web, including buy-one-get-one-free coupons and free samples on food, beauty products, and more. Brandie does her best to test the samples herself, so you know the offers are legit.

- Visit FreeSamplesBlog.com for information about free product samples, coupons, and giveaways happening at stores nationwide.

- At DailyEDeals.com/free_stuff, freebies are sorted by free product samples; free merchandise such as T-shirts, gift cards, and cosmetics; free after rebate; and offers to make easy money. Some of these links are more reputable than others, but it's definitely worth a look.

- If you're looking for a great, all-around site to find lots of different kinds of freebies, try Freebies4Mom.com. Heather, the mom who runs the site, finds coupons and free samples from around the web and posts them daily. Recent finds include a free luxury bathrobe from Dove, free Pampers diapers, buy-one-get-one-free coupons for Snapple, and more.

- TotallyFreeStuff.com has so many links to freebies it's hard not to be overwhelmed! They gather everything here, so if you look for freebies on a daily basis this is a good site to find offers you didn't find elsewhere.
- YoFreeStuff.com specializes in links to free gift cards, household products, food samples, and pie-in-the sky freebies like big screen TVs (which often require you to make purchases online or sign up friends for junk mail).
- At 1MyFreebies.com there is an ever-changing array of free offers, every day! Check back often for free offers that range from free candy to free photos at Sears Portrait Studio, and more.

Facebook Fan Pages

If you're already on Facebook, you've probably "liked" various companies, organizations, bands, TV shows, and random funny pages. If you're not already on Facebook, it's time to give in to your friends and family members who have been urging you to join! It's a great way to stay in touch, but it's also a great way to stay apprised of free stuff that is being offered by the companies you love. Once you've signed up for Facebook, find the companies that make products you use regularly by typing each one's name into Facebook's search bar. Many companies—like Burger King, Babies "R" Us, Wheat Thins, Origins, Walgreens, and more—offer coupons and freebies just for "liking" their page. And don't worry, it's easy. All you have to do is go to the company's page and click the button that says "like" (naturally).

Sometimes, It's as Easy as Asking

Here's a secret not many people know: companies want to give you their products for free. More specifically, their new products that they're hoping you'll tell all your friends about. Keep your eyes open for new types of candy, cosmetics, soda, and snack foods. Visit the company's website or look on the product's label to find the company's address. Write a letter (which usually works much better than an email) saying how interested you are in the product, and ask if you can have a free sample. For faster processing, write the name of the product on the outside of the envelope. Below is a letter you can use yourself—just fill in the names!

Dear [Company Name],

I've always enjoyed your products, so I was really excited to hear about [name of product]. Since I'm on a tight budget, I was hoping you'd be willing to send me a free sample to try and share with my friends. Thank you so much for your time and consideration.

Sincerely,

[Your name and address]

Join Twitter

If you're like us, even the word "twitter" makes you feel a little overwhelmed. But even if you're not interested in sending 140-character messages to your friends, Twitter.com is a great site for finding freebies, sales, and other bargains—fast. After you've chosen a username and password, then what do you do? First, check sites you normally frequent (and the ones listed in this chapter). Many will have a link that says "Follow us on Twitter!" Click the link and then the "follow" button, and these sites will now be in your "feed." (Don't forget to add WhoKnewTips for the or art, type "writing contests" or "art contests," for instance, into a search engine to find even more opportunities.

- Check for exclusions. Many contests will exclude people from a certain state. These left-out states are your gain (assuming you don't live in one!), because if fewer people can enter, your chances of winning will go up. Also look for contests with particularly high age requirements or that are just for one gender.

- Bookmark sites of contests you can enter again. Use your internet browser or a bookmark-site like Delicious.com to keep track of contests that allow you to enter more than once. Many allow a click a day, and some give something away each week and restart. If you have a lot of sites to keep track of, try organizing them in folders based on how much you want the prize or how often you can enter.

- Avoid any contests you think a lot of people will enter. Remember, the name of the game is trying to up your chances of winning by lowering the number of contestants. If a sweepstakes has been advertised heavily or has a really long entry period, avoid it. Likewise, if you find a contest held by a local business or that has a short entry period, your chances will go up.

- Only enter contests you trust. When entering a contest, you should never have to enter credit card information or your social security number. It's best to only enter contests from companies or sites you recognize.

latest from our site, WhoKnewTips.com!) For ideas for other sites to follow, type "freebie," "sale," or "bargain" into Twitter's search bar. You'll find there's a dazzling array of free offers available from thousands of sites. Again, click on the username and the "follow" to add to your feed, and you'll soon have a custom-made list of discounts at your fingertips. If all of this still sounds too overwhelming, there's yet another option. Go to CheapTweet. com, which compiles freebie, bargain, and discount offers from around the Twitter community.

Sweepstakes Secrets

Who doesn't love a good contest? Instead of buying a lottery ticket each week, put yourself in the running to win big by spending a little time each day or week entering online sweepstakes. Here are some tips to help you get that new car/ exotic vacation/lifetime supply of beef jerky of your dreams.

- Make an email address just for contests. When entering many contests, you are also signing up for a lifetime of junk mail. Just make sure to sift through the junk carefully in case you're notified of a win! It's usually pretty easy to tell the difference.
- The biggest, best source for contests around the web is Online-Sweepstakes.com, which has sweepstakes organized by type, new, and expiring soon.
- If you're only interested in the really big bucks and prizes, visit HelpingMomsConnect.com/contests.htm. The great thing about the links on this site is you normally don't have to do anything to win—just sign up.
- For smaller contests that often require you to submit something or comment on a site, try ContestGuide.com and ContestForMoms.com. If you have a special talent like writing